Apostolic Training Manual

Introduction to Apostolic Ministry

Understanding the Role and Function of Apostolic Ministers

DR. DWAYNE C. PERRY

ML Excellence Publishing

DEDICATION

To the dreamers who were told their dreams were too big;

To the ones who were labeled as insignificant;

To the ones who were deemed unworthy of success;

This dedication is for you.

You refused to let the opinions of others define you. You held onto the promises of God with unwavering faith. You embraced the whispers of destiny that stirred within your soul;

This dedication is for you.

In the face of doubt and discouragement, you chose to rise above the limitations imposed on you. You dared to believe that God's plans for you were greater;

This dedication is for you.

To the ones who were told they would never make it; to the ones who were pushed aside and forgotten; to the ones who were told they were not enough;

This dedication is for you.

For in your weakness, God's strength was made perfect. In your brokenness, God's healing power was revealed. In your perseverance, God's faithfulness shined brightly;

This dedication is for you.

May this dedication serve as a reminder, that you are seen, valued, and loved by the Creator, and your worth is not determined by the opinions of others;

This dedication is for you.

May you continue to walk in the truth of God's promises; May you rise above every obstacle and limitation; May you inspire others with your unwavering faith;

This dedication is for you. To those who have been counted out and overlooked, yet believed in what God said about you;

This dedication is for you!

With love and admiration,

Dr. Dwayne C. Perry

INTRODUCTION

Apostolic training plays a crucial role in equipping individuals for effective ministry and leadership within the Church. As the need for apostolic ministry continues to grow in the 21st century, it becomes imperative to develop a comprehensive course and textbook on apostolic training.

This book aims to highlight the reasons behind creating such a resource and the potential impact it can have on individuals, churches, and the advancement of the Kingdom of God. One of the primary reasons for creating a course and textbook on apostolic training is the scarcity of comprehensive resources available on this subject. While there are numerous resources on general ministry training, there is a significant gap when it comes to specific apostolic training. By developing a course and textbook, we are addressing this void.

Apostolic leaders are essential for the growth and expansion of the Church. They carry a unique anointing and gifting to establish and strengthen churches, plant new ones, and advance the Kingdom of God. However, many aspiring apostolic leaders lack access to formal training and mentorship opportunities. This resource provides them with the necessary tools, knowledge, and practical insights to fulfill their calling effectively, while equipping them to navigate the challenges, develop their character, and operate in the authority and anointing of apostles.

Apostolic ministry finds its roots in the New Testament Church. However, there is often a lack of clarity and understanding regarding the biblical foundation of apostolic ministry. By creating a course and textbook, we can establish a solid biblical foundation for apostolic training. This resource will delve into the role of apostles in the early Church, their qualifications, the apostolic commission, and their ministry functions. It will provide a comprehensive understanding of apostolic ministry based on the teachings and examples found in the Scriptures.

Apostolic ministry is not meant to be carried out in isolation but in partnership with other ministries and leaders. By creating this training resource, we can emphasize the importance of teamwork, collaboration, and healthy relationships within apostolic teams. We will provide practical guidance on building and nurturing apostolic relationships, establishing effective governance structures, and fostering unity among diverse ministries. This training will equip individuals to work together towards a common vision and purpose, promoting the advancement of the Kingdom of God.

Apostolic ministry is not limited to a select few but is meant to impact the entire Body of Christ. This resource will provide guidance on integrating apostolic training into the local church context, developing an apostolic culture, and implementing training programs. As individuals are equipped and empowered through this resource, they will be able to bring transformation and growth to their local churches, communities, and beyond.

Creating a course and textbook on apostolic training is essential to meet the growing need for equipping apostolic leaders, establishing a biblical foundation, promoting unity and collaboration, and impacting the local church and beyond. This resource will provide individuals with the necessary knowledge, practical insights, and spiritual formation to fulfill their apostolic calling effectively. By investing in apostolic training, we can contribute to the advancement of the Kingdom of God and the growth of the Church in the 21st century.

This training involves the impartation of knowledge, skills, and spiritual guidance necessary for fulfilling the Great Commission. Both scripture and theologians emphasize the significance of apostolic training in preparing believers for their calling. Let us explore this importance, drawing from quotes by theologians and scriptural references.

FOREWORD

As you embark on this apostolic journey through the pages of this Apostolic Training Manual, allow Dr. Perry's wisdom, ministerial insight, and experiences to inspire and empower you. His biblical insight of the scripture, apostolic anointing, and dedication to serving the Lord and developing people, will undoubtedly leave a lasting impact on your life. Prepare to be challenged, motivated, and equipped as you study the transformative teachings of this Apostolic Training Manual.

ML Excellence Publications

COURSE ONE
Understanding Apostolic Ministry

Chapter 1. Importance of Training

Apostolic training is essential for equipping individuals to fulfill their ministry callings. Theologian John Stott once said, "The church is not an institution to be served but a people to be equipped."9 This quote highlights the purpose of apostolic training, which is to equip believers for effective service in the body of Christ.

Scripture also emphasizes the importance of equipping for ministry. In Ephesians 4:11-12, the apostle Paul writes, "And he gave the apostles, the prophets, the evangelists, the shepherds, and teachers, to equip the saints for the work of ministry, for building up the body of Christ." This passage underscores the role of apostolic training in preparing believers for their ministry responsibilities and the edification of the church.

Apostolic training is not only about acquiring knowledge but also about spiritual formation and character development. Theologian Dallas Willard once said, "Discipleship is the process of becoming who Jesus would be if he were you."14 This quote emphasizes that apostolic training involves the transformation of individuals into the likeness of Christ. Scripture affirms the importance of spiritual formation. In Romans 12:2, the apostle Paul writes, "Do not be conformed to this world, but be transformed by the renewal of your mind, that by testing you may discern what is the will of God, what is good and acceptable and perfect." This verse highlights the need for a renewed mind and transformed character, which is fostered through apostolic training.

Apostolic training prepares individuals to be commissioned for service in advancing the Kingdom of God. Theologian John Wesley once said, "Give me one hundred preachers who fear nothing but sin and desire nothing but God, and I care not whether they be clergymen or laymen, they alone will shake the gates of Hell and set up the kingdom of Heaven upon Earth."[12] This quote emphasizes the impact of well-trained apostolic ministers in fulfilling the Great Commission.

Scripture also emphasizes the commissioning of believers for service. In Matthew 28:19-20, Jesus says, "Go therefore and make disciples of all nations, baptizing them in the name of the Father and of the Son and of the Holy Spirit, teaching them to observe all that I have commanded you." This passage highlights the mandate for all believers to be trained and sent out to make disciples, which is facilitated through apostolic training. Apostolic training holds great importance in equipping individuals for ministry, fostering spiritual formation, and commissioning believers for service. The insights of theologians, along with scriptural references, emphasize the significance of this training in fulfilling the Great Commission and building up the body of Christ. By investing in apostolic training, believers can be equipped to effectively serve and impact the world for the glory of God.

Chapter 2. Biblical Foundation for Apostolic Ministry

Biblical Apostolic Ministry refers to a specific form of ministry that is rooted in the teachings and practices of the early apostles as recorded in the Bible. It is characterized by a focus on the foundational teachings of Jesus Christ, the establishment and growth of the Church, and the equipping and sending forth of believers to fulfill the Great Commission.

In the New Testament, the term "apostle" refers to those who were chosen and commissioned by Jesus Himself to be His witnesses, to establish and oversee churches, and to carry the message of the Gospel to the world. The apostles played a crucial role in the early Church, providing leadership, teaching, and guidance to believers.

In the ever-evolving landscape of ministry and leadership, it is crucial to establish a firm biblical foundation for apostolic ministry. With its unique calling and anointing, this ministry plays a vital role in the growth and expansion of the Church. However, without a solid understanding of its biblical roots, it can become distorted or diluted. This section highlights the significance of establishing biblical foundations for apostolic ministry and the impact it can have on the Church and its mission.

Apostolic ministry finds its roots in the New Testament Church, where apostles were foundational leaders who carried a distinct anointing and authority. However, over time, the understanding and practice become varied and sometimes disconnected from its biblical origins. By emphasizing the need for biblical foundations, we can preserve the identity and purpose of the ministry. This ensures that apostolic leaders operate in alignment with the biblical model, carrying the authority and anointing necessary for effective ministry.

Firstly, the lack of clarity regarding the qualifications, functions, and limitations of apostolic ministry can lead to abuses of authority or the promotion of unscriptural practices. By grounding apostolic ministry in the Scriptures, we can guard against these distortions and excesses. A thorough understanding of these biblical principles provides a framework for discernment and accountability, ensuring that apostolic leaders operate within the boundaries set by God's Word.

To be clear, apostolic ministry is not merely a title or position; it is a calling to serve and equip the Church for the work of the ministry. Without a biblical foundation, apostolic leaders may rely on personal experiences, cultural trends, or popular teachings to guide their practice. However, the Scriptures provide a comprehensive guide for apostolic ministry, outlining the functions, roles and responsibilities of apostles. We will revisit these in chapter five.

By grounding apostolic practice in the Word of God, leaders can ensure that their ministry aligns with God's purposes and leads to the edification and growth of the Church. When rooted in biblical foundations, this ministry has the potential to bring significant impact to the Church and its mission. By studying and applying the biblical principles of apostolic ministry, leaders can tap into the same anointing and authority that empowered the early apostles. This strengthens their impact on the Church, leading to transformation, growth, and the fulfillment of the Great Commission. When grounded in biblical foundations, apostolic ministry becomes a unifying force within the Body of Christ, bridging denominational divides and fostering collaboration among diverse ministries. This unity strengthens the Church's witness and impact, as it reflects the love of Christ to a divided world. As apostolic leaders embrace their biblical calling, the Church will experience greater growth, power, and impact for the glory of God.

Chapter 3. Elements, History & Power of the Apostolic

Biblical Apostolic Ministry has several key elements:

1) A commitment to the authority and sufficiency of the Bible as the inspired Word of God, serving as the foundation for all teaching, doctrine, and practice.

2) A central emphasis on the message of the Gospel, proclaiming the good news of salvation through faith in Jesus Christ and His redemptive work on the cross. A central focus on the discipleship and equipping of believers to live out their faith, grow in spiritual maturity, and fulfill their God-given purpose and calling.

3) A commitment to the establishment and growth of healthy, biblically grounded churches that reflect the values and teachings of the early apostolic Church.

4) A belief in and expectation of the ongoing work of the Holy Spirit, including the gifts of the Spirit, miracles, healing, and the demonstration of God's power in the lives of believers and in the ministry of the Church.

5) The recognition of apostolic leaders who provide oversight, guidance, and accountability to churches and ministries, modeling servant leadership and equipping others for ministry.

6) A commitment to fulfilling the Great Commission by actively engaging in evangelism, missions, and reaching the lost with the message of Jesus Christ.

History of the Apostolic Ministry

The Apostolic Ministry has a rich history that spans both the Old and New Testaments. While the term "apostle" may not always be explicitly used, the concept of individuals being sent by God with authority and commission to represent Him and establish His kingdom can be found throughout Scripture. Let us explore this history in more detail, along with relevant scriptural references.

The Old Testament shares examples of individuals sent by God to fulfill specific purposes and establish His kingdom. One notable figure is Moses. Sent by God to deliver the Israelites from slavery in Egypt, Moses performed signs and wonders, received divine revelation, and established the foundation for the nation of Israel. Through him, God demonstrated His power and authority (Exodus 3-4, Exodus 7-12).

Another example is the twelve spies sent by Moses to explore the Promised Land. Although not called apostles, twelve leaders were sent as representatives of the people and brought back a report of what they saw. This mission had a significant impact on the future of the Israelites (Numbers 13:1-33). Additionally, the prophets in the Old Testament functioned similarly to the apostles. They were sent by God to deliver His messages, call the people to repentance, and establish His kingdom on earth. Prophets like Isaiah, Jeremiah, and Ezekiel also played crucial roles in God's plan for His people.

In the New Testament, apostolic ministry takes on a more prominent role with the arrival of Jesus Christ, the ultimate apostle sent by God the Father. Jesus selected twelve apostles to be His closest disciples, whom He sent out to preach the Gospel, heal the sick, and perform miracles. These apostles included Peter, James, John, and others (Matthew 10:1-4, Mark 3:13-19, Luke 6:12-16). After Jesus' ascension, the twelve apostles continued His ministry and played a vital role in establishing the early church. They preached the Gospel, performed signs and wonders, and provided leadership and guidance to the believers. The book of Acts provides numerous accounts of their apostolic ministry, including the selection of Matthias to replace Judas Iscariot (Acts 1:12-26, Acts 2:42-47, Acts 5:12-16). Paul, although not one of the original twelve apostles, was called by Jesus Himself to be an apostle to the Gentiles. He planted numerous churches, wrote many epistles, and played a significant role in spreading the Gospel and establishing the early Christian community. His apostolic ministry is well-documented in the book of Acts and his epistles (Acts 9:1-19, Acts 13-28,1 Corinthians 9:1-2).

Alongside the twelve apostles and Paul, other individuals such as Barnabas and Silas were recognized as apostolic ministers. They were sent out on specific missions, preached the Gospel, and played essential roles in the expansion of the early church (Acts 11:19-30, Acts 15:22-35, Acts 16:19-40).

In summary, the biblical history of apostolic ministry in the Old and New Testaments reveals a consistent pattern of individuals being sent by God with authority and commission to represent Him and establish His kingdom. While the term "apostle" may not always be used, the concept and function of apostolic ministry can be seen throughout Scripture.

The Power of Apostolic Ministry

Biblical Apostolic Ministry holds immense power and significance in the advancement of God's Kingdom. It involves the proclamation of the Gospel, the establishment of churches, and the equipping of believers for effective service. Both scripture and theologians emphasize the power and impact of apostolic ministry, providing guidance and inspiration for those called to this important role.

Let us explore this power, drawing from quotes by theologians and scriptural references. First, theologian John Stott, in his book "The Preacher's Portrait," writes, "The power of the gospel is not in the messenger, nor in the recipient, but in the message itself."[9] This quote highlights that the power of apostolic ministry lies in the message of the Gospel, which could bring about radical transformation.

Scripture also emphasizes the power of the Gospel. In Romans 1:16, the apostle Paul writes, "For I am not ashamed of the gospel, for it is the power of God for salvation to everyone who believes." This verse underscores the inherent power of the Gospel to bring salvation to all who receive it. Additionally, in 1

Corinthians 1:18, Paul writes, "For the word of the cross is folly to those who are perishing, but to us who are being saved it is the power of God." This passage highlights the transformative power of the message of the cross.

Apostolic ministry involves the establishment and nurturing of churches, which serve as beacons of light and agents of transformation in their communities. Theologian Dietrich Bonhoeffer, in his book "Life Together," writes, "The church is the church only when it exists for others."[1] This quote emphasizes that the power of apostolic ministry lies in the selfless service and impact of the church in the world.

Much of Scripture affirms the power of the church. In Matthew 16:18, Jesus says, "And I tell you, you are Peter, and on this rock I will build my church, and the gates of hell shall not prevail against it." This verse highlights the power and authority of the church, which stands firm against the forces of darkness. Additionally, in Ephesians 3:10, Paul writes, "so that through the church the manifold wisdom of God might now be made known to the rulers and authorities in the heavenly places." This passage emphasizes that the church serves as a testimony to the wisdom and power of God.

In addition, apostolic ministry involves the equipping of believers for effective service and ministry. Scripture emphasizes the importance of mandate. In Ephesians 4:11-12, Paul writes, "And he gave the apostles, the prophets, the evangelists, the shepherds, and teachers, to equip the saints for the work of ministry, for building up the body of Christ."

Clearly, biblical apostolic ministry holds great power and significance in the advancement of God's Kingdom. The insights of theologians, along with scriptural references, emphasize the transformative power of the Gospel, the impact of the church, and the importance of equipping believers. By embracing the power of apostolic ministry, believers can effectively proclaim the Gospel, establish churches, and equip others for service, ultimately bringing glory to God and advancing His Kingdom on earth.

Chapter 4. Jesus' Perspective on the Apostolic

The Intentional Selection

Jesus' perspective on apostolic ministry holds a significant place in the Christian faith, and its foundations can be traced back to the teachings and actions of Jesus Christ Himself. He provides valuable insights into the ministry's purpose, authority, and mission. Let us explore these foundations, supported by relevant scriptural references.

Jesus handpicked twelve apostles to be His closest disciples and sent them out with a specific mission. In Mark 3:13-14, we read, "And he went up on the mountain and called to him those whom he desired, and they came to him. And he appointed twelve (whom he also named apostles) so that they might be with him and he might send them out to preach."

This passage highlights Jesus' intentional selection of the apostles and their dual role: to be with Him and to be sent out by Him. It emphasizes the authority bestowed upon them by Jesus Himself, as they were chosen to represent Him and continue His work on earth. One of the primary purposes of apostolic ministry is to proclaim the Gospel message. In Matthew 10:7-8, Jesus instructs His apostles, saying, "And proclaim as you go, saying, 'The kingdom of heaven is at hand.' Heal the sick, raise the dead, cleanse lepers, cast out demons. You received without paying; give without pay." Here, Jesus commissions the apostles to preach the message of the kingdom of heaven, accompanied by signs and wonders.

They were to freely share the good news, demonstrating the power and authority of God through miraculous acts. This commission to preach the Gospel remains a foundational aspect of apostolic ministry.

The Establishment of the Church

Jesus' perspective on apostolic ministry also includes the establishment and building of the Church. In Matthew 16:18, Jesus declares, "And I tell you, you are Peter, and on this rock, I will build my church, and the gates of hell shall not prevail against it." This statement reveals Jesus' intention to establish His Church, with the apostles playing a crucial role in its foundation. They were entrusted with the responsibility of leading and shepherding the early Christian community, ensuring its growth and spiritual well-being.

The sending of the Holy Spirit was prophesied by Jesus before His ascension. He promised to send the Holy Spirit to empower and guide the apostles in their ministry. In Acts 1:8, Jesus says, "But you will receive power when the Holy Spirit has come upon you, and you will be my witnesses in Jerusalem and in all Jerusalem, Judea. Samaria, and to the end of the earth." This promise of the Holy Spirit's indwelling and empowerment underscores the divine enablement necessary for apostolic ministry.

In conclusion, the biblical foundations of apostolic ministry, as seen from Jesus' perspective, reveal its calling, authority, purpose, and mission. Jesus intentionally chose and commissioned the apostles, granting them authority to represent Him and continue His work. They were called to preach the Gospel, establish the Church, and were promised the empowering presence of the Holy Spirit. These foundations provide a solid framework for understanding the significance and role of apostolic ministry in the Christian faith.

Other Key Biblical References

The Biblical Foundations of Apostolic Ministry can be found throughout the New Testament, particularly in the teachings and actions of Jesus Christ and the writings of the apostles. Here are some key biblical foundations of Apostolic Ministry.

Jesus personally chose and commissioned twelve apostles to be His witnesses and to carry out His ministry on earth (Matthew 10:1-4, Mark 3:13-19, Luke 6:12-16). He gave them authority to heal the sick, cast out demons, and proclaim the Kingdom of God (Matthew 10:7-8, Mark 6:7-13). Before ascending to heaven, Jesus gave the Great Commission to His apostles, instructing them to go and make disciples of all nations, baptizing them and teaching them to obey His commands. (Matthew 28:18-20, Mark 16:15-18, Acts 1:8).

The apostles played a central role in teaching and establishing the early Church. They were entrusted with the task of passing on the teachings of Jesus and the revelation of the Gospel (Acts 2:42, Ephesians 2:20, 1 Corinthians 3:10-11). They demonstrated the power of the Holy Spirit through signs, wonders, and miracles, confirming the message of the Gospel (Acts 2:43, Acts 5:12, Acts 8:6-7, 2 Corinthians 12:12).

Also, the apostles were instrumental in planting and overseeing churches in various regions. They appointed elders and leaders, provided guidance and correction, and ensured the soundness of doctrine and practice (Acts 14:23, Titus 1:5, 1 Peter 5:1-4). Their role in equipping and sending out believers for ministry was key to the expansion of the early church. They imparted spiritual gifts, trained, and mentored leaders, and sent out missionaries to spread the Gospel (Ephesians 4:11-13, 2 Timothy 2:2, Acts 13:1-3).

The apostles carried a unique authority and anointing in their ministry. They were recognized as foundational leaders in the Church, and their teachings and writings became the basis for the New Testament Scriptures (2 Corinthians 10:8, 2 Peter 3:15-16).

These biblical foundations provide a framework for understanding Apostolic Ministry. It involves carrying out the Great Commission, teaching and equipping believers, planting and overseeing churches, demonstrating the power of the Holy Spirit, and operating in apostolic authority. Apostolic Ministry seeks to follow the example of the early apostles in their commitment to the teachings of Jesus, the empowerment of the Holy Spirit, and the advancement of the Kingdom of God.

Chapter 5. Role and Function of the Apostle

According to the Bible, apostolic ministers have a unique role and function within the Church. Here are some key aspects of these responsibilities, as outlined in the Scriptures.

Apostolic Ministers are foundational in nature, playing a crucial role in establishing and laying the groundwork for the Church. They are likened to master builders who lay the foundation of Jesus Christ (1 Corinthians 3:10-11, Ephesians 2:20). Their ministry involves imparting the teachings of Jesus, establishing sound doctrine, and providing a solid spiritual foundation for believers. Apostolic ministers have a responsibility to equip and mentor believers for ministry. They are called to train and raise up leaders, impart spiritual gifts, and provide guidance and support for the growth and development of individuals and the Church as a whole (Ephesians 4:11-13, 2 Timothy 2:2).

Another function of apostolic ministers involves planting and overseeing churches. They have a role in establishing new works, appointing leaders, and providing oversight and guidance to ensure the health and growth of the local church (Acts 14:23, Titus 1:5, 1 Peter 5:1-4).

In addition, apostolic ministers are responsible for proclaiming the Gospel and making disciples of all nations. They have a passion for evangelism and missions, actively engaging in spreading the message of Jesus Christ and advancing the

Kingdom of God (Matthew 28:18-20, Mark 16:15-18, Acts 1:8). In doing so, they operate in the power of the Holy Spirit, demonstrating signs, wonders, and miracles. They have a supernatural anointing to heal the sick, cast out demons, and bring deliverance to those in need (Acts 2:43, Acts 5:12, Acts 8:6-7, 2 Corinthians 12:12).

Moreover, apostolic ministers have a responsibility to guard and uphold sound doctrine. They are vigilant in protecting the purity and integrity of the Gospel, ensuring that the teachings and practices align with the Scriptures (1 Timothy 4:6, 2 Timothy 1:13-14, Titus 1:9).

A primary quality of apostolic ministers is the exemplification of servant leadership. They lead with humility, love, and a heart of service, putting the needs of others before their own (Matthew 20:25-28, 1 Peter 5:2-3). It is important to note that the role and function of apostolic ministers may vary in different contexts and seasons. However, these biblical principles provide a foundation for understanding their calling and purpose within the Church.

Importance of a Firm Foundation

Since apostolic ministers are instrumental in establishing, equipping, and advancing the Kingdom of God, being anchored by a firm foundation is imperative. Jesus taught that a strong foundation is essential for withstanding the storms of life and building a life that is pleasing to God. Both scripture and theologians affirm the significance of a firm foundation, providing guidance and inspiration for believers. Let us explore., drawing from quotes by theologians and scriptural references.

First, in Matthew 7:24-27, Jesus shares the parable of the wise and foolish builders. He says, "Everyone then who hears these words of mine and does them will be like a wise man who built his house on the rock. And the rain fell, and the floods came, and the winds blew and beat on that house, but it did not fall, because it had been found on the rock. And everyone who hears these words of mine and does not do them will be like a foolish man who built his house on the sand. And the rain fell, and the floods came, and the winds blew and beat against that house, and it fell, and great was the fall of it." This parable highlights the importance of building our lives on a solid foundation, which is hearing and obeying the words of Jesus. Theologian Charles Spurgeon, in his book "The Treasury of David," writes, "The rock is the truth of God, the sure and everlasting foundation upon which the soul may build its eternal hopes."[10] This quote emphasizes that the foundation Jesus speaks of is the truth of God's Word.

Jesus also emphasized the foundation of faith in Him as the cornerstone. In Matthew 16:18, Jesus says to Peter, "And I tell you, you are Peter, and on this rock I will build my church, and the gates of hell shall not prevail against it." Theologian John Calvin, in his book "Institutes of the Christian Religion," writes, "Christ is the only foundation of the Church, and that the ministry of the Word is the only means of establishing it."[2] This verse highlights that Jesus Himself is the foundation upon which the Church is built.

Also, theologian A.W. Tozer, in his book "The Pursuit of God," writes, "The foundation of all true knowledge of God must be a clear mental apprehension of His perfections as revealed in Holy Scripture."[11]

Jesus taught that the foundation of our relationship with Him is love and obedience. In John 14:23, Jesus says, "If anyone loves me, he will keep my word, and my Father will love him, and we will come to him and make our home with him." Theologian John Wesley, in his book "The Works of John Wesley," writes, "Love is the fulfilling of the law, the end of the commandment."[12] This verse emphasizes that love for Jesus is demonstrated through obedience to His teachings.

The foundation of our relationship with Him is built on love and obedience. Theologian Dietrich Bonhoeffer, in his book "The Cost of Discipleship," writes, "Only he who believes is obedient, and only he who is obedient believes." [1]

In conclusion, the insights of theologians, along with scriptural references, provide guidance and inspiration for believers to establish a firm foundation in their relationship with Jesus. By building our lives on this foundation, we can withstand the storms of life and live in a way that is pleasing to God.

Workbook 1:

Introduction to Apostolic Ministry Training

Instructions: Answer the following questions by selecting the correct option or writing a short essay response. For multiple-choice questions, choose the best answer. For true or false questions, mark either "True" or "False." The answer key is provided at the end of the manual.

1. What does the term "Apostolic" refer to?

a) A specific religious denomination

b) The teachings of the apostles

c) The role of bishops in the church

d) The study of ancient manuscripts

2. True or False: The Apostolic Age refers to the time period immediately following the death and resurrection of Jesus Christ.

3. Who was the first apostle chosen by Jesus?

a) Peter

b) John

c) James

d) Andrew

4. What is the significance of the apostles in Christianity?

a) They were the first followers of Jesus.

b) They were chosen to spread the teachings of Jesus.

c) They were witnesses to the resurrection of Jesus.

d) All of the above

5. True or False: The apostles were given the authority to perform miracles and heal the sick.

6. What is the role of apostolic succession in the church?

a) It ensures the continuity of apostolic teachings and authority.

b) It guarantees salvation for believers.

c) It establishes a hierarchical structure within the church.

d) It is a historical record of the apostles' travels.

7. Who is considered the "Apostle to the Gentiles"?

a) Peter

b) James

c) Paul

d) John

8. True or False: The apostles wrote the majority of the New Testament.

9. What is the significance of the Day of Pentecost in relation to the apostles?

a) It marked the beginning of their ministry.

b) It was when they received the Holy Spirit.

c) It was when they performed their first miracle.

d) All of the above

10. Define the term "apostolic doctrine."

11. True or False: The apostles faced persecution and martyrdom for their faith.

12. Who was the apostle who betrayed Jesus?

a) Peter

b) John

c) James

d) Judas Iscariot

13. What is the role of apostles in the modern-day church?

14. True or False: The apostles were eyewitnesses to the life, death, and resurrection of Jesus.

15. Name three apostles mentioned in the New Testament, apart from the twelve disciples.

16. Define the term "apostolic authority."

17. True or False: The apostles were given the power to forgive sins.

18. What is the significance of the Council of Jerusalem in relation to the apostles?

19. Explain the concept of apostolic succession and its importance in various Christian traditions.

20. True or False: The apostles were given the Great Commission to go and make disciples of all nations.

COURSE TWO
Characteristics of the Apostolic

Chapter 1. Key Characteristics Identified

Apostolic ministry holds a unique and vital role within the Church, serving as a catalyst for growth, expansion, and transformation. Understanding the characteristics of apostolic ministry is essential for aspiring leaders seeking to fulfill their calling and make a significant impact in the Kingdom of God.

This section aims to explore the key characteristics of apostolic ministry and their significance in equipping leaders for effective service.

One of the primary characteristics of apostolic ministry is a pioneering spirit. Apostles are called to venture into uncharted territories, breaking new ground for the Gospel and establishing the Kingdom of God. They possess a vision and passion to reach the unreached, plant churches, and bring transformation to communities. This pioneering spirit enables apostolic leaders to embrace risk, overcome obstacles, and lead with courage and faith. By understanding and cultivating this characteristic, aspiring apostolic leaders can effectively navigate the challenges and uncertainties of ministry.

Apostolic ministry is also marked by a unique authority and anointing. Apostles are entrusted with a divine commission to govern, guide, and equip the Church. They carry a spiritual authority that is not based on position or title but on their intimate relationship with God and their alignment with His purposes. This authority empowers apostolic leaders to bring about change, confront spiritual strongholds, and release the Kingdom of God in their spheres of influence. Understanding and operating in this authority and anointing is crucial for apostolic leaders to fulfill their calling effectively.

To continue, apostolic ministry is not limited to personal accomplishments but is focused on equipping and mobilizing others for ministry. Apostles have the heart to see believers equipped, empowered, and released into their God-given callings and giftings. They invest in the development of leaders, imparting wisdom, knowledge, and practical skills.

Equally as important, apostolic leaders understand the importance of raising up a new generation of leaders who can carry the vision and mission forward. By embracing this characteristic, apostolic leaders can create a lasting impact by multiplying their influence through others.

Because ministry thrives on building relationships and networks, apostles understand the power of collaboration, unity, and partnership in advancing the Kingdom of God. They actively seek to build bridges between churches, ministries, and leaders, fostering a sense of community and shared vision. Apostolic leaders prioritize relationship-building, recognizing that the collective strength of the Body of Christ is greater than individual efforts. By cultivating this characteristic, apostolic leaders can create a network of support, encouragement, and accountability that enhances their effectiveness in ministry.

To continue, apostolic ministry requires adaptability and flexibility in response to the ever-changing needs and contexts of the Church and society. Apostles are not bound by rigid structures or traditions but are willing to embrace new methods, strategies, and cultural expressions to effectively reach and disciple people. They are sensitive to the leading of the Holy Spirit and are open to divine redirection. This characteristic enables apostolic leaders to navigate cultural, social, and technological shifts, ensuring that the Gospel remains relevant and impactful in every generation.

Understanding the characteristics of apostolic ministry is crucial for aspiring leaders seeking to fulfill their calling and make a significant impact in the Kingdom of God. The pioneering spirit, authority, anointing, equipping, and mobilizing, building relationships and networks, and adaptability and flexibility are key characteristics that define apostolic ministry. These characteristics reflect Jesus' perspective on apostolic ministry and provide a framework for understanding the qualities that should be present in those called to this role. Let us explore these characteristics, supported by relevant scriptural references.

To begin, two of the most profound characteristics of apostolic ministers are humility and servanthood. Jesus emphasized the importance of humility and servanthood as foundational characteristics of apostolic ministry. In Mark 10:45, Jesus says, "For even the Son of Man came not to be served but to serve, and to give his life as a ransom for many." This verse highlights Jesus' own example of humility and selfless service. (We will discuss these two virtues in-depth later.) Apostolic ministers are called to follow in His footsteps,

26

prioritizing the needs of others above their own. They are to serve with a humble heart, imitating Jesus' sacrificial love and compassion.

Next, Apostolic ministers must possess unwavering faith and trust in God. Jesus often commended individuals for their faith and encouraged His disciples to trust in God's provision. In Matthew 17:20, Jesus says, "Truly, I say to you, if you have faith like a grain of mustard seed, you will say to this mountain, 'Move from here to there,' and it will move, and nothing will be impossible for you." This verse highlights the power of faith and the limitless possibilities that come with trusting in God. Apostolic ministers are called to have faith that moves mountains, believing in God's ability to accomplish the impossible through them.

Importantly, Jesus' ministry was characterized by love and compassion for all people. He taught His disciples to love one another and to show compassion to those in need. In John 13:34-35, Jesus says, "A new commandment I give to you, that you love one another: just as I have loved you, you also are to love one another. By this, all people will know that you are my disciples if you have love for one another." This passage emphasizes the importance of love as a distinguishing characteristic of apostolic ministry. Apostolic ministers are called to love others unconditionally, just as Jesus loved His disciples. Their love should be a testimony to the world, revealing their identity as followers of Christ.

In addition, apostolic ministers must exhibit boldness and courage in proclaiming the Gospel and standing for truth. Jesus encouraged His disciples not to fear but to boldly testify about Him. In Luke 12:8, Jesus says, "I tell you, everyone who acknowledges me before men, the Son of Man also will acknowledge before the angels of God." This verse highlights the importance of boldly proclaiming Jesus' name and teachings.

Apostolic ministers are called to be courageous in sharing the Gospel, even in the face of opposition or persecution. They are to stand firm in their convictions, unafraid to speak the truth.

Jesus' perspective on apostolic ministry includes a focus on discipleship and equipping others for ministry. He invested time and energy in training His disciples, preparing them to carry on His work. In Matthew 28:19-20, Jesus says, "Go therefore and make disciples of all nations, baptizing them in the name of the Father and of the Son and of the Holy Spirit, teaching them to observe all that I have commanded you." This passage highlights the importance of discipleship and the responsibility of apostolic ministers to train and equip others. They are called to teach and mentor, helping believers grow in their faith and empowering them to fulfill their own ministry callings.

The characteristics of apostolic ministers, as seen from Jesus' perspective, reflect His teachings and example.

These characteristics include:

a. Humility – Philippians 2:5-8

b. Servanthood – Matthew 23:11

c. Faith – 2 Corinthians 5:7

d. Love – John 13:35

e. Compassion – Matthew 9:36

f. Boldness – 2 Timothy 1:7

f. Courage – Ephesians 6:10

g. Discipleship – Matthew 28:19-20

h. Equipping the saints – Ephesians 4:11-13

By embodying these qualities, apostolic ministers can effectively represent Jesus Christ and fulfill their calling to advance His kingdom on earth.

According to Scripture, apostolic ministers exhibit certain characteristics that are essential to their role and function within the Church. These characteristics were displayed by Jesus Christ and were taught to the disciples who became the Apostles and founders of the first-century church.

Here are some key characteristics of Apostolic ministers as outlined in the Bible:

1. Called and Commissioned: Apostolic ministers are called and commissioned by God for their specific ministry. They have a clear sense of divine calling and are obedient to fulfill the purpose and mission entrusted to them (Acts 9:15, Galatians 1:1).

2. Anointed and Empowered: Apostolic ministers operate in the power and anointing of the Holy Spirit. They rely on the Spirit's guidance, enabling, and empowering to carry out their ministry effectively (Acts 1:8, 1 Corinthians 2:4).

3. Faithful and Diligent: Apostolic ministers are faithful and diligent in their service to God and His people. They are committed to their calling, persevering through challenges and obstacles, and remaining steadfast in their devotion to God (1 Corinthians 4:2, 2 Timothy 2:2).

4. Teachable and Humble: Apostolic ministers have a teachable spirit and humility. They are open to correction, willing to learn from others, and recognize their dependence on God's wisdom and guidance (Proverbs 11:2, James 4:6).

5. Bold and Courageous: Apostolic ministers exhibit boldness and courage in proclaiming the Gospel and standing for truth. They are not afraid to confront opposition, persecution, or cultural pressures, but instead rely on God's strength and conviction (Acts 4:13, Acts 4:29-31).

6. Visionary and Strategic: Apostolic ministers have a vision for the advancement of the Kingdom of God. They possess strategic thinking and planning skills, seeking God's guidance to implement His purposes and strategies (Proverbs 29:18, Acts 16:9- 10).

7. Discerning and Wise. Apostolic ministers demonstrate discernment and wisdom in their decision-making and leadership. They rely on the Holy Spirit's guidance to discern God's will and make sound judgments (1 Corinthians 2:6-7, James 1:5).

8. Relational and Shepherd-hearted: Apostolic ministers have a heart for people and a desire to shepherd and care for God's flock. They build relationships, provide pastoral care, and nurture the spiritual growth and well-being of those under their care (1 Peter 5:2-3, Ephesians 4:11-13).

9. Committed to Sound Doctrine: Apostolic ministers are committed to upholding and teaching sound doctrine. They are diligent in studying and accurately interpreting Scripture, ensuring that their teaching aligns with the truth of God's Word (Titus 1:9, 2 Timothy 2:15).

These God given apostolic characteristics serve as a guide for apostolic ministers to fulfill their calling and effectively carry out their ministry in preaching the Gospel and leading the church. These qualities and virtues are necessary for leading, equipping, and advancing the Kingdom of God, according to the teachings and example of Jesus Christ and the first apostles, who were the leaders of the first century church.

Chapter 2. Spiritual Maturity and Personal Holiness

Spiritual maturity and personal holiness are foundational aspects of Christian discipleship and essential for effective ministry. Aspiring leaders must recognize the significance of cultivating spiritual maturity and pursuing personal holiness in their lives. This section aims to explore the importance of these concepts, their interconnection, and their role in equipping leaders for impactful ministry.

To begin, spiritual maturity refers to the process of growing and developing in one's relationship with God, characterized by a deepening understanding of His Word, a vibrant prayer life, and a surrendered heart. It involves the transformation of one's character, attitudes, and behaviors to reflect the image of Christ. Spiritual maturity is not solely based on knowledge or age but is marked by a genuine and intimate connection with God. It enables leaders to discern God's will, navigate challenges, and make wise decisions rooted in biblical truth. Spiritual maturity equips leaders to effectively shepherd and disciple others, providing guidance and support in their spiritual journeys.

Next, personal holiness is closely intertwined with spiritual maturity and refers to a life set apart for God's purposes. It involves consecration, purity, and obedience to God's commands. Personal holiness requires a commitment to live in alignment with God's Word, allowing the Holy Spirit to transform every aspect of one's life. It encompasses moral integrity, ethical conduct, and a pursuit of righteousness. Personal holiness is not a legalistic adherence to rules but a response to God's grace and a desire to honor Him in all areas of life. Leaders who prioritize personal holiness serve as examples to others, inspiring them to pursue a deeper relationship with God and live lives that reflect His character.

Spiritual maturity and personal holiness are intricately connected. Spiritual maturity is the result of a life dedicated to personal holiness, while personal holiness is nurtured and strengthened through the process of spiritual maturity. As leaders grow in their understanding of God's Word, engage in prayer and worship, and surrender to the work of the Holy Spirit, they are transformed into vessels of holiness.

Likewise, as leaders pursue personal holiness, they deepen their relationship with God, growing in spiritual maturity. The interconnection between spiritual maturity and personal holiness creates a solid foundation for leaders to effectively serve and minister to others. Spiritual maturity and personal holiness are essential for equipping leaders for effective ministry. Leaders who prioritize spiritual maturity are better equipped to discern God's leading, navigate challenges, and make decisions that align with His will. They possess a depth of understanding and wisdom that enables them to effectively teach, counsel, and shepherd others. Leaders who pursue personal holiness exhibit integrity, authenticity, and a genuine love for God and people. Their lives become a testimony of God's transforming power, drawing others to Christ, and inspiring them to pursue a deeper relationship with Him. Together, these two characteristics equip leaders to lead with humility, grace, and compassion, fostering an environment of growth and discipleship within their ministries.

This training will delve into the importance of spiritual maturity and personal holiness, providing students with the necessary knowledge, practical tools, and spiritual formation to cultivate these qualities in their lives. Theologians and the Bible provide valuable insights into these topics, offering guidance and encouragement for those seeking to deepen their relationship with God. Let us explore these concepts, drawing from quotes by theologians and scriptural references.

First, theologian John Stott once said, "Maturity is the capacity to endure uncertainty."[9] This quote highlights the importance of perseverance and trust in God's faithfulness as we navigate the uncertainties of life. Scripture also emphasizes the significance of spiritual maturity. In Ephesians 4:13, the apostle Paul writes, "until we all attain to the unity of the faith and of the knowledge of the Son of God, to mature manhood, to the measure of the stature of the fullness of Christ." This verse underscores the goal of spiritual maturity, which is to become more like Christ in our thoughts, attitudes, and actions.

To continue, personal holiness refers to the pursuit of a life set apart for God's purposes. Theologian A.W. Tozer once said, "Holiness, as taught in the Scriptures, is not based upon knowledge on our part. Rather, it is based upon the resurrected Christ in- dwelling us and changing us into His likeness."[11] This quote emphasizes that personal holiness is not merely a result of our efforts but is a work of God's transforming power within us.

The Bible consistently emphasizes the call to personal holiness. In 1 Peter 1:15-16, the apostle Peter writes, "But as he who called you is holy, you also be holy in all your conduct, since it is written, 'You shall be holy, for I am holy.'" This passage highlights the divine mandate for believers to pursue holiness, as it reflects the character of God Himself.

Both spiritual maturity and personal holiness involve the process of sanctification, which is the ongoing work of the Holy Spirit in conforming believers to the image of Christ. Theologian J.I. Packer once said, "Sanctification is the process of becoming more like Christ in our conduct and character."[8] This quote emphasizes that sanctification is a lifelong journey of growth and transformation. Scripture affirms the process of sanctification. In 2 Corinthians 3:18, the apostle Paul writes, "And we all, with unveiled face, beholding the glory of the Lord, are being transformed into the same image from one degree of glory to another. For this comes from the Lord who is the Spirit." This verse highlights that sanctification is a progressive work, as we continually behold the glory of the Lord and allow His Spirit to transform us.

Moreover, the Bible places a strong emphasis on spiritual maturity and personal holiness as essential aspects of the Christian life. Here are some key teachings from Scripture regarding these topics:

Spiritual Maturity

- **Growing in Knowledge and Understanding:** Believers are encouraged to grow in their knowledge and understanding of God's Word, developing a deeper relationship with Him (2 Peter 3:18, Colossians 1:9-10).

- **Renewing the Mind:** Christians are called to renew their minds and be transformed by the Holy Spirit, aligning their thoughts and attitudes with God's truth (Romans 12:2, Ephesians 4:23-24).

- **Bearing Spiritual Fruit:** Spiritual maturity is evidenced by the bearing of spiritual fruit, such as love, joy, peace, patience, kindness, goodness, faithfulness, gentleness, and self-control (Galatians 5:22-23, John 15:5).

- **Discernment and Wisdom:** Mature believers can discern between good and evil, and they seek wisdom from God to make godly decisions (Hebrews 5:14, James 1:5).

Personal Holiness

- **Set Apart for God:** Believers are called to be holy and set apart for God's purposes. They are to live a life that reflects God's character and values (1 Peter 1:15-16, 2 Corinthians 6:17-18).

- **Pursuing Righteousness:** Christians are encouraged to pursue righteousness and flee from sin. They are to live in obedience to God's commands and strive for moral purity (1 Timothy 6:11, 1 Peter 2:11).

- **Sanctification:** The process of sanctification involves being transformed into the likeness of Christ. It is a lifelong journey of becoming more like Him in character and conduct (Romans 8:29, 2 Corinthians 3:18).

- **Walking in the Spirit:** Believers are called to walk in the power and guidance of the Holy Spirit, allowing Him to lead and empower them to live holy lives (Galatians 5:16, Romans 8:13).

The Bible teaches that spiritual maturity and personal holiness are not achieved through human effort alone but are the result of the work of the Holy Spirit in the lives of believers. It is a cooperative process where believers actively participate in their growth and transformation, relying on God's grace and power. Through prayer, studying God's Word, fellowship with other believers, and obedience to His commands, Christians can grow in spiritual maturity and pursue personal holiness, ultimately reflecting the image of Christ to the world.

Scripture repeatedly emphasizes the importance of personal holiness as a prerequisite for encountering God. In Matthew 5:8, Jesus declares, "Blessed are the pure in heart, for they shall see God." This verse highlights the connection between personal holiness and the ability to perceive and experience the presence of God.

Furthermore, Hebrews 12:14 states, "Strive for peace with everyone, and for the holiness without which no one will see the Lord." This passage underscores the necessity of personal holiness in our pursuit of God. Without a commitment to holiness, our spiritual vision becomes clouded, hindering our ability to truly see and experience God's presence. Personal holiness not only enables us to encounter God but also transforms us into His likeness. Theologian John Wesley, known for his emphasis on personal holiness, believed that holiness is the work of God's grace in our lives, leading to a transformation of character and conduct. Wesley's theology of sanctification emphasizes the ongoing process of being made holy by the work of the Holy Spirit.[12] This transformative process involves surrendering our lives to God, allowing Him to purify our hearts and conform us to the image of Christ. Through personal holiness, we become vessels through which God's love and righteousness are manifested in the world.

The pursuit of personal holiness requires intentional effort and a desire to align our lives with God's standards. Theologian A.W. Tozer, known for his writings on the pursuit of God, believed that personal holiness is not an optional aspect of the Christian life but an essential part of our relationship with God. Tozer writes, "Holiness, as taught in the Scriptures, is not based upon knowledge on our part. Rather, it is based upon the resurrected Christ in-dwelling us and changing us into His likeness." [11] This perspective highlights the transformative work of God's Spirit within us, enabling us to pursue personal holiness and experience a deeper communion with God. As we strive for personal holiness, we open ourselves to a deeper encounter with God and become vessels through which His love and righteousness are manifested in the world.

Chapter 3. Servant Leadership and Humility

Servant leadership and humility are foundational principles that shape the character and effectiveness of Christian leaders. In a world that often values power, prestige, and self-promotion, understanding and embracing the concepts of servant leadership and humility are crucial for aspiring leaders in ministry. Servant leadership is a leadership style rooted in the example of Jesus Christ, who came not to be served but to serve (Mark 10:45). It is characterized by a selfless and sacrificial attitude, a genuine concern for the well-being of others, and a commitment to meeting their needs. Servant leaders prioritize the growth, development, and empowerment of those they lead, seeking to serve rather than be served. They lead with humility, compassion, and a servant's heart, modeling Christ-like behavior and inspiring others to do the same. Servant leadership fosters an environment of trust, collaboration, and unity, enabling the flourishing of individuals and the advancement of the Kingdom of God.

Humility is a foundational virtue that underpins servant leadership. It is the recognition of one's own limitations, weaknesses, and dependence on God. Humility involves a posture of surrender, acknowledging that all gifts, talents, and achievements come from God's grace. Humble leaders do not seek to exalt themselves or seek personal gain but instead prioritize the needs and well-being of others. They are open to feedback, willing to learn from others, and quick to give credit to those they lead.

Servant leadership and humility are deeply interconnected. Servant leadership requires humility as its foundation, as leaders must first recognize their own need for God's grace and guidance. Humility allows leaders to set aside their own agendas, egos, and desires for power, and instead focus on the needs and growth of those they lead. Conversely, servant leadership cultivates humility, as leaders continually seek to serve others, recognizing that their role is not about personal gain or recognition but about advancing God's Kingdom and bringing glory to Him. The interconnection between servant leadership and humility creates a powerful force that transforms leaders and impacts those they serve.

In addition, servant leadership and humility are essential for equipping leaders for effective ministry. Leaders who embrace servant leadership prioritize the growth, development, and empowerment of those they lead. They create an environment where individuals can thrive, utilizing their gifts and talents for the Kingdom of God. Servant leaders inspire and motivate others, fostering a sense of ownership and shared vision within their ministries. Humble leaders, on the other hand, create a safe and authentic space for individuals to grow and flourish. They lead with vulnerability, acknowledging their own weaknesses and mistakes, and creating a culture of grace and forgiveness. Servant leadership and humility equip leaders to lead with integrity, compassion, and a genuine desire to serve others, resulting in effective ministry that impacts lives and transforms communities. These foundational principles shape the character and effectiveness of Christian leaders.

Understanding and embracing these concepts is crucial for aspiring leaders in ministry. The interconnection between servant leadership and humility creates a powerful synergy that transforms leaders and impacts those they serve.

This section will delve into the significance of servant leadership and humility, providing students with the necessary knowledge, practical tools, and spiritual formation to cultivate these qualities in their lives. By embracing servant leadership and humility, leaders can effectively serve, inspire, and empower others, bringing glory to God and advancing His Kingdom.

Both scripture and theologians emphasize the significance of servant leadership and humility, providing guidance and inspiration for those in leadership positions. Let us explore these qualities, drawing from quotes by theologians and scriptural references. To begin, theologian Robert K. Greenleaf, in his book "Servant Leadership: A Journey into the Nature of Legitimate Power and Greatness," writes, "The servant-leader is servant first... It begins with the natural feeling that one wants to serve, to serve first."[4] This quote highlights the foundational principle of servant leadership, which is the desire to serve others.

Scripture also emphasizes the importance of servant leadership. In Mark 10:45, Jesus says, "For even the Son of Man came not to be served but to serve, and to give his life as a ransom for many." This verse exemplifies Jesus' own servant leadership, as He came to serve and sacrifice Himself for the salvation of humanity.

Humility is a key characteristic of servant leadership, involving a modest and selfless attitude. Theologian C.S. Lewis, in his book "Mere Christianity," writes, "Humility is not thinking less of yourself, but thinking of yourself less."[5] This quote highlights that humility is not about diminishing oneself but rather redirecting focus away from self and towards others. Scripture further affirms the importance of humility. In Philippians 2:3-4, the apostle Paul writes, "Do nothing from selfish ambition or conceit, but in humility count others more significant than yourselves. Let each of you look not only to his own interests but also to the interests of others." This passage emphasizes the call to humility, considering others as more important and prioritizing their needs.

The ultimate example of servant leadership and humility is found in the life and ministry of Jesus Christ. Theologian Henri Nouwen, in his book "In the Name of Jesus: Reflections on Christian Leadership," writes, "The leader is the one who must lead us into the unknown, toward a future that is not yet realized... The leader is the one who must take the first step into the unknown."[7] This quote highlights that servant leaders, like Jesus, are willing to step into the unknown and lead by example. Scripture also presents Jesus as the epitome of servant leadership and humility. In John 13:14-15, Jesus says, "If I then, your Lord and Teacher, have washed your feet, you also ought to wash one another's feet. For I have given you an example, that you also should do just as I have done to you." This passage demonstrates Jesus' act of humility in washing the disciples' feet and His call for them to follow His example.

Servant leadership and humility are crucial qualities for effective leadership in the Kingdom of God. The insights of theologians, along with scriptural references, emphasize the significance of these qualities in leadership. By embracing servant leadership and cultivating humility, leaders can exemplify the character of Christ and effectively serve and lead others. Here are some key teachings from the Bible regarding these principles:

Jesus as the Ultimate Example:

- Jesus Himself modeled servant leadership and humility throughout His earthly ministry. He washed the disciples' feet, stating that He came not to be served but to serve (John 13:1-17, Matthew 20:28).

- Jesus taught that the greatest among His followers would be the one who humbles themselves and becomes like a servant (Matthew 23:11-12).

Humility as a Virtue:

- Scripture repeatedly emphasizes the importance of humility. It is described as a virtue that pleases God and leads to exaltation (Proverbs 22:4, James 4:10).

- Humility involves recognizing our dependence on God, acknowledging our limitations, and having a proper view of ourselves in light of God's greatness (Philippians 2:3-4, Romans 12:3).

Servant Leadership:

- Jesus taught that leadership in His Kingdom is characterized by serving others. He instructed His disciples to lead by example, just as He did, and to serve one another in love (Matthew 20:25-28, Mark 10:42-45).

- Servant leaders prioritize the needs of others, seek to empower, and equip them, and are willing to sacrifice their own interests for the sake of those they lead (1 Peter 5:2-3, Galatians 5:13). 4. The Call to Humility and Servanthood:

- Believers are called to imitate Christ's humility and adopt a servant's heart. They are encouraged to consider others as more important than themselves and to serve one another in love (Philippians 2:5-8, Galatians 5:13).

- Humility and servanthood are to be demonstrated in all areas of life, including relationships, work, and ministry (Ephesians 4:2, Colossians 3:12-13).

Rewards of Humility and Servant Leadership:

- Scripture teaches that God exalts the humble and rewards those who serve faithfully. Humility and servant leadership are honored by God and bring blessings and favor (Luke 14:11, James 4:6).

In summary, Scripture teaches that servant leadership and humility are essential qualities for believers. By following the example of Jesus, adopting a servant's heart, and humbly serving others, Christians can reflect the character of Christ and impact the world around them.

Chapter 4. Visionary and Strategic Thinking

Visionary and strategic thinking are essential qualities for effective leadership in the Kingdom of God. They involve the ability to see beyond the present circumstances, discern God's direction, and develop a plan to fulfill His purposes. Both scripture and theologians emphasize the significance of visionary and strategic thinking, providing guidance and inspiration for leaders. Let us explore these qualities, drawing from quotes by theologians and scriptural references.

First, visionary thinking involves the ability to see beyond the immediate and envision a future aligned with God's purposes. Theologian John Maxwell, in his book "The 21 Irrefutable Laws of Leadership," writes, "A leader is one who knows the way, goes the way, and shows the way."[6] This quote highlights the importance of leaders having a clear vision and being able to communicate and lead others towards that vision. Scripture also emphasizes the importance of visionary thinking. In Proverbs 29:18, it says, "Where there is no vision, the people perish." This verse underscores the need for leaders to have a vision that inspires and guides the people they lead. Additionally, in Jeremiah 29:11, God says, "For I know the plans I have for you, declares the Lord, plans for welfare and not for evil, to give you a future and a hope." This verse reminds us that God is a visionary God who has plans and purposes for His people.

Next, strategic thinking involves the ability to develop and implement plans that align with the vision and goals of an organization or ministry. Theologian Peter Drucker, in his book "The Effective Executive," writes, "The best way to predict the future is to create it."[3] This quote emphasizes the importance of leaders taking intentional and strategic actions to shape the future.

Scripture also affirms the importance of strategic thinking. In Luke 14:28, Jesus says, "For which of you, desiring to build a tower, does not first sit down and count the cost, whether he has enough to complete it?" This verse highlights the need for careful planning and strategic thinking before embarking on any endeavor. Additionally, in Proverbs 16:3, it says, "Commit your work to the Lord, and your plans will be established." This verse reminds us that strategic thinking should be grounded in seeking God's guidance and aligning our plans with His will.

In addition, the biblical account of Nehemiah provides a powerful example of visionary and strategic thinking. Nehemiah had a vision to rebuild the walls of Jerusalem and strategically planned and executed the project. Theologian Warren Wiersbe, in his book "Be Determined: Standing Firm in the Face of Opposition," writes, "Nehemiah was a man of prayer, but he was also a man of action."[13] This quote highlights Nehemiah's combination of visionary thinking and strategic action. Scripture also presents Nehemiah as an example of visionary and strategic thinking. In Nehemiah 2:17, Nehemiah shares his vision with the people, saying, "You see the trouble we are in, how Jerusalem lies in ruins with its gates burned. Come, let us build the wall of Jerusalem, that we may no longer suffer derision."

This verse demonstrates Nehemiah's ability to cast a compelling vision. Additionally, throughout the book of Nehemiah, we see his strategic planning and execution in mobilizing the people, overcoming obstacles, and completing the project. While the Bible does not explicitly use the terms "visionary" and "strategic thinking," it does provide principles and examples that can guide believers in these areas. Here are some biblical teachings that relate to visionary and strategic thinking:

Seeking God's Guidance:

- Proverbs 3:5-6 encourages believers to trust in the Lord with all their hearts and lean not on their own understanding. This implies the need to seek God's guidance and wisdom in making decisions and formulating plans.

God's Plans and Purposes:

- Jeremiah 29:11 states that God has plans for His people, plans to prosper them and not to harm them, plans to give them hope and a future. This suggests that believers should align their vision and strategies with God's purposes.

Strategic Planning:

- Proverbs 21:5 teaches that the plans of the diligent lead to profit. This implies the importance of strategic thinking and planning to achieve desired outcomes.

Vision and Prophetic Guidance:

- Proverbs 29:18 states that where there is no vision, the people perish. This suggests the importance of having a clear vision and direction for individuals and communities.
- The Bible also contains examples of individuals like Joseph, Daniel, and Nehemiah who had a clear vision and strategic plans to fulfill God's purposes in their respective contexts.

Seeking God's Kingdom:

- Matthew 6:33 instructs believers to seek first the kingdom of God and His righteousness. This implies that visionary and strategic thinking should be centered on advancing God's kingdom and promoting His righteousness.

Dependence on the Holy Spirit:

- Acts 1:8 teaches that believers will receive power when the Holy Spirit comes upon them. This suggests the need for reliance on the Holy Spirit's guidance and empowerment in formulating and executing visionary and strategic plans. While the Bible does not provide a detailed framework for visionary and strategic thinking, it encourages believers to seek God's guidance, align their plans with His purposes, and rely on the Holy Spirit's empowerment. By doing so, believers can develop a visionary mindset and strategic approach that aligns with God's will and brings glory to Him.

Chapter 5. Discernment and Wisdom

Discernment and wisdom are essential qualities for effective leadership in the Kingdom of God. They involve the ability to make sound judgments, understand God's will, and navigate complex situations with spiritual insight. Both scripture and theologians emphasize the significance of discernment and wisdom, providing guidance and inspiration for leaders. Let us explore these qualities, drawing from quotes by theologians and scriptural references.

To begin, discernment is the ability to distinguish between truth and falsehood, right and wrong, and to perceive the leading of the Holy Spirit. Theologian A.W. Tozer, in his book "The Pursuit of God," writes, "The spiritual man is... a man of spiritual judgment. He is able to appraise things, to judge them, to tell the difference between one thing and another, between things that differ."[11] This quote highlights the importance of discernment in the life of a believer and a leader.

Scripture also emphasizes the significance of discernment. In 1 John 4:1, it says, "Beloved, do not believe every spirit, but test the spirits to see whether they are from God, for many false prophets have gone out into the world." This verse encourages believers to exercise discernment and test the teachings and spirits they encounter. Additionally, in Hebrews 5:14, it says, "But solid food is for the mature, for those who have their powers of discernment trained by constant practice to distinguish good from evil." This passage highlights the need for believers to develop their discernment through constant practice and spiritual growth.

Next, wisdom is the ability to apply knowledge and understanding in a way that aligns with God's truth and purposes. Theologian J.I. Packer, in his book "Knowing God," writes, "Wisdom is the power to see, and the inclination to choose, the best and highest goal, together with the surest means of attaining it."[8] This quote emphasizes that wisdom involves not only knowledge but also the ability to make wise choices considering God's truth. Scripture affirms the importance of wisdom. In Proverbs 4:7, it says, "The beginning of wisdom is this: Get wisdom, and whatever you get, get insight." This verse highlights the value of wisdom and encourages believers to actively seek it. Additionally, in James 1:5, it says, "If any of you lacks wisdom, let him ask God, who gives generously to all without reproach, and it will be given him." This passage reminds us that wisdom is a gift from God, and we can seek His guidance and wisdom in all aspects of life.

The biblical account of King Solomon provides a powerful example of discernment and wisdom. When God offered Solomon anything he desired, Solomon asked for wisdom to govern God's people. Theologian Charles Spurgeon, in his book "The Treasury of David," writes, "Solomon's choice of wisdom was the best that could have been made."[10] This quote highlights the significance of Solomon's request and the importance of wisdom in leadership.

Scripture also presents Solomon as an example of discernment and wisdom. In 1 Kings 3:9, Solomon prays to God, saying, "Give your servant, therefore, an understanding mind to govern your people, that I may discern between good and evil, for who is able to govern this your great people?" This verse demonstrates Solomon's desire for discernment and wisdom to lead God's people effectively. Additionally, throughout the book of Proverbs, Solomon's wisdom is evident in his teachings and insights on various aspects of life. By cultivating discernment, seeking God's guidance, and applying wisdom in decision-making, leaders can navigate challenges, make sound judgments, and fulfill God's purposes in their leadership roles.

The Bible places a high value on discernment and wisdom, emphasizing their importance in the life of a believer. Here are some key teachings from Scripture regarding discernment and wisdom:

Seeking Wisdom:

- Proverbs 4:7 states that wisdom is supreme and encourages believers to seek wisdom above all else. It is portrayed as a valuable treasure that brings understanding and guidance.

The Source of Wisdom:

- James 1:5 teaches that if anyone lacks wisdom, they should ask God, who gives generously to all without finding fault. God is the ultimate source of wisdom, and believers are encouraged to seek His guidance and understanding.

Discerning Good and Evil:

- Hebrews 5:14 speaks of the importance of discernment, stating that mature believers have their powers of discernment trained to distinguish good from evil. Discernment enables believers to make wise choices and avoid deception.

The Role of the Holy Spirit:

- 1 Corinthians 2:12-14 teaches that the Holy Spirit enables believers to understand and discern spiritual truths. The Spirit reveals God's wisdom to believers, guiding them in making wise decisions.

The Fear of the Lord:

- Proverbs 9:10 states that the fear of the Lord is the beginning of wisdom. The fear of the Lord involves reverence, awe, and obedience to God, and it is the foundation for acquiring true wisdom and discernment.

Testing the Spirits:

- 1 John 4:1 instructs believers to test the spirits to see whether they are from God. This involves discerning between true and false teachings, examining the motives and actions of others, and discerning the leading of the Holy Spirit.

Seeking Counsel:

- Proverbs 11:14 advises seeking wise counsel, recognizing that in the multitude of counselors there is safety. Seeking the input and wisdom of others can provide valuable perspectives and insights.

Walking in Wisdom:

- Ephesians 5:15-17 encourages believers to walk in wisdom, making the most of every opportunity and understanding the Lord's will. Wisdom enables believers to live purposefully and make wise choices in their daily lives. Discernment and wisdom are not merely intellectual abilities but spiritual gifts that come from God.

By seeking God's wisdom, relying on the Holy Spirit, and applying biblical principles, believers can develop discernment and wisdom to navigate life's challenges, make wise decisions, and honor God in all they do.

Workbook 2:

Characteristics of Apostolic Ministers

Instructions: Answer the following questions by selecting the correct option or writing a short essay response. For multiple-choice questions, choose the best answer. For true or false questions, mark either "True" or "False." The answer sheet is provided at the end of the manual.

1. What are the characteristics of apostolic ministers?

a) Humility, servant leadership, and boldness

b) Wealth, power, and authority

c) Intelligence, eloquence, and charisma

d) Ritualistic practices, deep spirituality, and isolation

2. True or False: Apostolic ministers are primarily focused on building their own personal empires.

3. What is the role of apostolic ministers?

a) To oversee the administration and finances of the church

b) To preach and teach the Word of God

c) To perform miracles and heal the sick

d) All of the above

4. What is the biblical foundation for apostolic ministry?

a) The teachings of the apostles in the New Testament

b) The Old Testament prophets

c) The writings of early church fathers

d) None of the above

5. True or False: Apostolic ministers are called to be accountable to a higher authority and to work in unity with other church leaders.

6. What is the significance of apostolic ministry in the modern-day church?

7. Define the term "apostolic anointing."

8. True or False: Apostolic ministers are exempt from facing challenges and hardships in their ministry.

9. What are some key qualities that apostolic ministers should possess?

10. Explain the concept of apostolic alignment and its importance in apostolic ministry.

11. True or False: Apostolic ministers are called to equip and empower others for ministry.

12. What is the role of apostolic ministers in advancing the Kingdom of God?

13. Define the term "apostolic authority."

14. True or False: Apostolic ministers are called to be examples of godly character and integrity.

15. Name three biblical figures who exemplify apostolic ministry.

16. Explain the concept of apostolic succession and its relevance to apostolic ministers.

17. True or False: Apostolic ministers are called to be visionaries and catalysts for change in the church.

18. What is the importance of spiritual covering in apostolic ministry?

19. Describe the relationship between apostolic ministry and the five-fold ministry mentioned in Ephesians 4:11-13.

20. True or False: Apostolic ministers are called to be ambassadors of Christ, representing Him and His kingdom on earth.

Workbook 1 Answer Key:

1. b) The teachings of the apostles

2. True

3. a) Peter

4. d) All of the above

5. True

6. a) It ensures the continuity of apostolic teachings and authority

7. c) Paul

8. True

9. d) All of the above

10. (Essay response required)

11. True

12. d) Judas Iscariot

13. (Essay response required)

14. True

15. (Essay response required)

16. (Essay response required)

17. True

18. (Essay response required)

19. (Essay response required)

20. True

Workbook 2 Answer Key:

1. a) Humility, servant leadership, and boldness

2. False

3. d) All of the above

4. a) The teachings of the apostles in the New Testament

5. True

6. (Essay response required)

7. (Essay response required)

8. False

9. (Essay response required)

10. (Essay response required)

11. True

12. (Essay response required)

13. (Essay response required)

14. True

15. (Essay response required)

16. (Essay response required)

17. True

18. (Essay response required)

19. (Essay response required)

20. True

About the Author

Apostle Dr. Dwayne C. Perry is the Senior Pastor of True Sanctuary of Praise Church, located in Riverview, FL., and is the husband of Prophetess Esther Marcellus-Perry. They have three adult children: Irving, Amber, and Cedric. He accepted the ministerial call on his life at the age of twenty-six.

He is also the founder of "The Academy at True Sanctuary of Praise," and the President of "Enhance Your Chance Community Development Center," which rehabilitates our young people, empowering them to be successful citizens.

Dr. Perry has been graced with the gift of empowering leaders to fulfill the total call of Jesus Christ on their lives. He has touched the lives of ministry leaders in many nations and is a sought-after speaker and motivator, who has the ability to connect with diverse audiences, making him a powerful force for change. He challenges individuals to overcome obstacles, embrace their unique gifts, and live a life of purpose and significance.

His life experiences as an athlete and in ministry have shaped his character and fueled his passion for making a positive impact. His unwavering commitment to serving others, combined with his natural leadership abilities, have positioned him as a catalyst for transformation and change in the lives of many people.

With a heart rooted in love and a deep desire to see others succeed, Dwayne serves with the heart of Christ, with a genuine love for people, uplifting and inspiring them through coaching, mentoring, writing, teachings, and ministry.

His journey has been marked by excellence, service, education, and a deep commitment to empowering others. With a career spanning 13 years as a professional basketball player, Dwayne's passion for sports and his dedication to ministry have shaped him into the person he is today.

Through his achievements as an athlete and ministerial teachings, Dwayne has touched countless hearts, unlocking their full potential and purpose. As a coach, mentor, and developer of people, he has made it his mission to help others in personal and professional growth. His commitment to nurturing talent and fostering a spirit of excellence has earned him the respect and admiration of many of his peers.

Dr. Perry is a servant leader who has the ability to see the potential in others, and his passion is empowering men, women, and youth for Kingdom purpose in Christ.

For more information on Apostle Dr. Dwayne C. Perry go to:

https://www.tsopchurch.org/

Notes

1. Bonhoeffer, Dietrich. *Life Together: The Classic Exploration of Christian Community*. Translated by John W. Doberstein, Harper One, 1954.

2. Calvin, John. *Institutes of the Christian Religion*. Translated by Henry Beveridge, Westminster John Knox Press, 1845.

3. Drucker, Peter F. *The Effective Executive*. Harper & Row, 1967.

4. Greenleaf, Robert K. *Servant Leadership: A Journey into the Nature of Legitimate Power and Greatness*. Paulist Press, 1977.

5. Lewis, C.S. *Mere Christianity*. HarperCollins, 2001.

6. Maxwell, John C. *The 21 Irrefutable Laws of Leadership: Follow Them and People Will Follow You*. Thomas Nelson, 1998.

7. Nouwen, Henri J. M. *In the Name of Jesus: Reflections on Christian Leadership*. Crossroad, 1989.

8. Packer, J. I. *Rediscovering Holiness: Know the Fullness of Life with God*. Rev. ed., Baker Books, 2009.

9. Stott, John. *Preacher's Portrait: Some New Testament Word Studies*. William B. Eerdmans Publishing Co., 1961.

10. Spurgeon, Charles H. *The Treasury of David, Vol. 1*. Passmore & Alabaster, 1865.

11. Tozer, A. W. *The Pursuit of God*. Christian Publications, 1948.

12. Wesley, John. *Sermons on Several Occasions*. The Methodist Conference Office, 1875.

13. Wiersbe, Warren W. *Be Determined: Standing Firm in the Face of Opposition*. David C Cook, 1995.

14. Willard, Dallas. *The Divine Conspiracy: Rediscovering Our Hidden Life in God*. Harper San Francisco, 1998.